LUNCH &
DINNER

&

COMFORT
FOOD

A
COLLECTION
OF
JAMAICAN
ORIGINAL RECIPES
WITH THE
LATEST JERK RECIPES
ADDED AND OTHER
FAMILY FAVORITES

BY WINNET BUCHANAN

To order additional copies of this book, contact:
Xlibris
844-714-8691
www.Xlibris.com
Orders@Xlibris.com

ISBN: Softcover   978-1-6698-1188-6
        EBook   978-1-6698-1187-9

Print information available on the last page

Rev. date: 02/26/2022

LUNCH & DINNER
& COMFORT FOOD

JAMAICAN STYLE FISH WITH ONIONS & PEPPERS:

King Fish Steaks or Whole Red Snapper

2-4 LBS. Fish (cut in steaks)	**1 Teaspoon Paprika**
1 Tablespoon Black Pepper	**2 eggs**
1 Teaspoon Season salt	**1 Cup Breadcrumbs**
1 Tablespoon Garlic Powder	**1 Medium Onion**
1 Lemon	

To Garnish: Onions, Red & Green Bell Peppers, Hot Cayenne Peppers & Vinegar

PREPARATION:

Wash fish with water and lime/lemon juice, dry thoroughly. Season with season salt, black pepper, sprinkle each slice with paprika. In a separate dish, slightly beat eggs add some salt and black pepper. Spread breadcrumbs on a sheet of paper. Dip the Fish slices in egg mixture and then bread crumb, coating slices well. Set aside on paper towel to dry coating. Heat oil in a Skillet; Fry the slices in hot oil on both sides until golden brown. Drain on paper towel to avoid fish soaking up oil. Arrange the fish on a platter and place in warm oven to keep ward.

(Cut very thin slices of sweet onions; red and green bell peppers; Optional choice, Cut Cayenne Peppers separately, set aside. In Separate Frying Pan Heat the ingredients, adding a dash of vinegar, until slightly sauté for 1 – 2 minutes. Garnish fish and add parsley and wedge of lemon on the side

JAMAICA ESCOVEITCHED FISH

Fish of choice: Goat Fish, King Fish Steaks, sliced ½" thick, Snapper, Jack fish

3 lbs. Fish	2 Cups malt vinegar (white or brown)
4 Teaspoon black pepper	½ cup oil for frying
4 Teaspoon salt	1 Teaspoon pimento seeds or whole allspice
½ scotch bonnet pepper	cut 2 Large Onions, sliced in strips
½ Teaspoon whole black pepper grains	½ Teaspoon dried Tabasco

PREPARATION:

Wash fish in water with lemon juice, or vinegar, Pat dry, lay on paper towels. Coat fish with combined salt, pepper and set aside.

Heat oil in frying pan to boiling point, fry fish on both sides until nice and crisp. Set aside in deep Pyrex dish or similar container. In separate saucepan combine vinegar, sliced onions, peppers, pimento seeds, whole black pepper grains and bring to a boil. Simmer until onions are tender, remove from heat to cool. Pour ingredients over fish and leave it to steep overnight, or for a couple of hours before serving. DELICIOUS!

JAMAICA BAKED FISH IN WINE

2-1/2 Lb. Fillet of Fish	2 Minced Shallots
A Few Slices of Lemon	1 Sm. Bottle Sliced Mushrooms
Sprig of Parsley	8-10 oz.
1 Whole unbroken green scotch	1 Teaspoon Lemon Juice
Bonnet Pepper	½ cup fresh sliced mushrooms
1 Clove of garlic	1 Tablespoon Brandy
1 Tablespoon flour	1 Tablespoon Butter/Margarine
¼ cup white wine to cover the fish;	Salt and pepper to taste

Place the fish in a baking dish. Add a few slices of onion; then 2 minced shallots; then mushroom; Add the dry white wine to cover the fish; 1 teaspoon lemon juice; a sprig of parsley; salt and pepper to taste; 1 clove garlic; and 1 green scotch bonnet pepper.

Bake in 350°F degrees oven for 20 to 30 minutes. Remove fish from oven; remove all the liquid and put it in a small saucepan. On top of stove boil liquid to about 1-1/4 cup. Warm a tablespoon of brandy in a ladle and light it, then pour the flaming brandy over the sauce. In a separate bowl, mix 1 tablespoon butter and flour; stir until it becomes thick and smooth. Add a pinch of cayenne pepper and stir into thickness. Pour the sauce mixture over the fish; sprinkle with parsley and arrange a few slices of lemon on top.

JERK FISH WITH CALALO, JAMAICAN STYLE

2 Whole Red Snapper

3 Onions

1 Teaspoon Paprika

1 unbroken green hot pepper

2 Tablespoon butter

1 lime/lemon

Jerk Seasoning

2 Tablespoon Jerk Sauce

1-1/2 lb. or bigger (leave the head on)

Dash of cayenne Pepper flakes

1 Teaspoon Black Pepper

1 Sweet pepper

2 level teaspoon ginger

3 cups chopped fresh Calaloo

1 Clove Garlic

Butter or Margarine

PREPARATION:

Wash fish thoroughly with lime or vinegar, dry and set aside.

Slice onion and sweet pepper into thin slices set aside. Sprinkle black pepper, garlic, salt, paprika and ground ginger on the fish, rub well into fish. Rub paprika and jerk sauce on the outside of the fish.

In a separate sauce pan, cook Calaloo until soft. Drain off water, then spoon into fish cavity, lay onion & pepper slices on top of calaloo and a sprig of fresh thyme. Add 2 tablespoon of butter or margarine on top and 3 tablespoons of water on foil. Wrap the fish in the foil and grill for ten minutes.

Add slices of pepper to your taste. or Bake in oven at 350ºF for 20-30 minutes. Remove from oven. Serve hot.

GRILLED SALMON

3 Lb. Salmon Fillet with the skin

½ Teaspoon Black pepper

4 Cloves fresh Garlic

2 Tb spoon fresh ginger (peeled and minced)

¾ Cup syrup (preferable pancake syrup)

½ Cup Vinegar

Lawyer's seasoned salt

3 Tablespoon Extra Virgin Olive Oil

sprigs of thyme

PREPARATIONS:

Brush olive oil over all of the salmon, then sprinkle Salmon with salt, & pepper. In separate container mix all ingredients together. Place Salmon on grill on Medium Heat. Skin side down. Grill for about 10 minutes. Add the rest of the ingredients on top and let grill for another 5-10 minutes then add the syrup. Rremove from grill and garnish with parsley. Serve with vegetables.

JAMAICAN STYLE CURRY GOAT

2-1/2 LBS. Goat Meat (cut in cubes)

3-4 cloves of Garlic

¼ Cup of Curry Powder

Few grains of Pimento grains (dried)

Few Sprigs of Thyme

Black Pepper

2 Medium Onions (white or yellow)

1 green Bell Pepper

4 Stalks Scallion (diced)

1 Scotch Bonnet Pepper

1 Teaspoon Lawry's Seasoned Salt

1 Tablespoon butter

PREPARATION:

Cut goat mean into 1-1/2" cubes, Rinse with water and a little vinegar. Season with season salt, black pepper, crushed garlic and Curry Powder diced onions and scallions, mixed in well. Let stand for at least ½ hour to marinate. Remove the seasoning and slightly brown in skillet with butter. Add about 1 pint of water and seasoning and allow to cook until tender, lastly add Scotch Bonnet pepper and simmer for about 10 minutes, Serve with par-boiled rice and vegetables of your choice. Do not let the mixture dry out. Add more water if needed to make enough gravy.

Option: Skip browning the meat, instead, add enough water to cover and stew until tender. Do not allow the water to completely dried out, leave enough liquid for gravy.

PAR BOILED RICE:

Use ½ lb. brown or white rice, rinse to remove starches, place in a pot that can cover tightly. Add enough water to cover the rice, add a pinch of salt and 1 tablespoon butter or margarine. Cover tightly, place on very low heat and let cook until rice grains are soft, or is light and fluffy. You can also use a rice cooker and follow the directions for the rice cooker.

JAMAICAN STYLE RICE AND KIDNEY BEANS/PEAS

3 Cups Parboil Rice

1 Med. Coconut (in shell)

2 Stalks of Scallion or leeks

1 whole green cayenne pepper

1 Qrt. Water

1 Cup Red Kidney Beans

2 Cloves Garlic

Few Sprigs of fresh Thyme

Salt to taste

PREPARATIONS:

Break coconut remove from shell, cut up in small pieces, put in blender with enough water turn the knob to grate. When the coconut juice is expressed, remove it from blender and strain the juice through a strainer into a container.

Place the coconut juice in a pot; add the Kidney Beans, garlic (crush the garlic with a rolling pin) add the salt. On medium heat, cook until peas is tender/or soft. (Test the beans by taking up a few grains in a spoon, it should be soft) Add Scallions, thyme and 1 whole cayenne pepper Note: do not cut or squish the pepper, it can be very hot)

Wash the rice and add to the pot. Make sure the water is sufficient to cover the rice. Cook on low heat until rice is soft. You may add a couple tablespoon of water to rice if needed until the rise is soft. Remove the pepper before stirring, remove from heat and serve hot.

JAMAICA REGGAE-STYLE PLANTAIN FRITTERS

2-3 Small Plantains (not very ripe)   1 Tablespoon Sugar

½ Teaspoon Baking Powder

Boil plantains, spread wax paper on cutting board and pound or mash the plantain, mix all ingredients together. Shape mixture into small mound and fry in very hot cooking oil. Remove from frying pan and place them on paper towels to absorb the oil .

JAMAICAN STYLE FRIED GREEN PLANTAINS

1 Lg. Green Plantain sliced in round thick slices. 1 Pint Cold water, mixed with 4 Tablespoon salt.

DIRECTIONS:

Steep plantain slices in the salted water for 1 hour. Heat skillet with sufficient oil to cover slices. Remove from water, pat dry with paper towels and fry lightly on both sides on medium heat. When slightly brown remove from heat and place on wax paper and roll each slice with a rolling pin until flattened. Return flattened pieces to frying pan brown until crisp. This makes an excellent cocktail snack.

BAKED PLANTAINS

Select well ripened plantains, not too soft. Slightly core the skin of each plantain, place them in foil wrap, and roll them in the wrap. Place in baking pan and bake for 30 minutes.

JAMAICA SALTED CODFISH FRITTERS

¼ Lb. Raw Codfish, (boneless)

1-1/2 Cup All Purpose Flour

Thyme

¼ teaspoon Baking Powder

¼ Teaspoon hot pepper flakes

1-1/2 Cups Cooking Oil

1 small onion

½ Teaspoon Paprika, or yellow Food Coloring

2 Stalks Scallion or Leeks

2 Medium size Plumb Tomatoes

or Black Pepper

1-1/2 Cup water

Pre-cook codfish in small pot, to remove most of the salt, remove from heat, and use a fork to separate into small pieces. Chop onions garlic, scallion or leeks, add hot pepper and tomatoes. Fry the chopped seasoning until cooked, remove from heat and set aside. In mixing bowl, add flour and a little water to make a mix similar to pancake mix, stir in codfish, and all the fried Seasoning and paprika.

Heat cooking oil in skillet. Spoon the batter into the hot oil, amount similar to a small pancake. Fry on both sides until golden brown. Remove from heat, set on paper towels to drain oil. Serve warm.

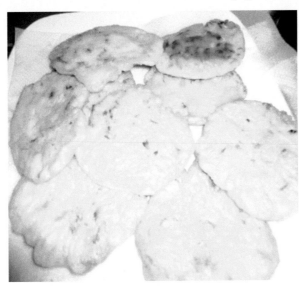

FRIED DUMPLINS OR JOHNNY CAKES

INGREDIENTS:

2 Cups All Purpose Flour

1 Tablespoon Baking Powder

¼ Teaspoon Salt

1 Tablespoon Margarine

½ Cup Milk

½ Cup Water

2 Cups cooking oil

DIRECTIONS:

Place Flour, salt, baking powder and margarine in bowl. Mix in well. Gradually add milk, mix or knead dough using your hand. Gradually add water until dough is thick but soft enough to make dumplings (not too dry) Cover with paper towel and set aside for 15 minutes. Allow the dough to rise a little. Pinch off pieces (enough to fit in the palm of your hands, about the size of a biscuit. Knead and flatten the dough, fry in hot oil, turning constantly on each side until brown. Remove from heat and place in a bowl with paper towels to absorb excess oil. Serve warm.

GINGERBREAD JAMAICAN STYLE

2-1/2 Cups All Purpose flour

1 Cup Brown Sugar

1 Cup Boiling Water

¼ Cup Melted Butter

1 Cup Molasses

3 Eggs

3 Teaspoon Ground Ginger (or grated fresh Ginger)

1 Teaspoon Mixed Spice

1 Teaspoon Baking Soda

1 Teaspoon Cinnamon

DIRECTIONS:

Cream eggs and sugar. Add melted butter, then molasses. Combine flour, baking soda, cinnamon, mixed spice and ginger to mixture, then add boiling water. Mixed together and pour into greased and floured baking tin. Bake at moderate temperature 350ºF for 20 minutes or until cooked, when knife is inserted in the center and it comes up dry.

JAMAICAN REGGAE-STYLE TURN CORNMEAL

2 Cups Cornmeal

6 Okras (sliced)

¼ Cup Diced Salt Fish (boneless)

4 Cups of coconut milk from 1 grated coconut

1 Medium onion (chopped)

1 lg. stalk Scallion (chopped)

Salad oil for frying seasoning

1 Small green pepper (diced)

1 Medium Tomato, diced

1/4 lb. Butter or Margarine

1 Teaspoon Black Pepper

Pepper (Optional)

Use sparingly cayenne pepper

(Note you could add 2 tablespoon diced salt pork) **Note: Cod fish and pork can be a bit salty, use salt sparingly. If you chose to use salt pork, fry until golden brown and discard oil. Set aside.**

Lightly fry onion, scallion, green sweet pepper, okras, tomato and hot pepper in small amount of cooking oil, combine with salt pork, salt fish/cod fish and butter, then add coconut milk and the black pepper.

Boil coconut milk separately until slight cream appears on surface, for around 10 to 15 minutes. Add cornmeal and stir well, cover and steam on low heat for approximately 25 minutes to half hour. (To steam: set pot in boiling water to cook).

JAMAICAN STYLE SPICY ROAST BEEF

SELECT A ROAST OF 5 LBS. DEPENDING ON THE SIZE OF THE PARTY.

1- Tablespoon Salt

1-1/2 Tablespoon Black Pepper

1 Tablespoon Dry Mustard

1-1/4 teaspoon Lawry's Seasoned salt

Few springs of Fresh Thyme

4 Cloves of Garlic, crushed

1-3/4 Cups Finely chopped carrots

2 Cups finely chopped celery

2 Cups finely chopped onions

1 Teaspoon Dry Oregano

2 Bay Leaves

1 tablespoon paprika

DIRECTIONS:

Wash beef thoroughly add a little vinegar to the water. With a sharp knife, make a few deep cuts, just enough to stuff some of the seasoning into the beef for good marinating.

Combine salt, pepper, mustard, ground thyme and cloves. Mix well and rub all over the meat on all sides. Stuff the fresh thyme, scallions and garlic cloves into the gashes. Place meat in a bowl and refrigerate overnight.

2nd DAY: Combine 4 cups of vinegar, salad oil and catsup and pour over meat. Place meat in oven covered at 300°F degrees for 20 minutes, uncover and base with the juice from the meat. Cook to desired taste. Remove meat from oven and allow it to cool.

In separate saucepan, combine brown gravy mix or beef gravy mix with slices of one onion, pepper and let simmer for a few minutes. Use an electric knife or a very sharp knife to slice beef. Serve with Rice or Potatoes and vegetables. Makes a delicious meal.

JAMAICAN STYLE SALTED COD FISH WITH ACKEES:

1 Can   (12 oz.) or 1 doz. Fresh Ackees, if available and cleaned.

½ Lb. Salted Cod Fish (remove bones and skin after it is cooked)

1/3 Cup Coconut Oil or Olive Oil

½ Teaspoon ground black pepper

¼ of a Scotch Bonnet pepper

3 Stalks Scallions (hopped)

4 Med. PlumTomatoes (diced)

3 Med. Size. Onions (chopped) fine)

DIRECTIONS:

Open can of Ackee. Rinse with cold water then put it in small pot and add a little water, enough to cover the Ackees. Let it cook for approximately 10 minutes. Remove from heat, drain off the water and set aside. Wash salted codfish, place in a pot, add sufficient water to cover codfish and let it boil for 20 minutes or until the fish is tender, rinse with cold water. Remove the skin and bones from the fish and flake with a fork and set aside.

In saucepan, fry all ingredients, onions, tomatoes, scallions, and pepper for 4-5 minutes or until tender. Add the Ackee and the fish and stir. Serve with rice or boiled green bananas.

Optional items. You could add fried and drained strips of crispy bacon if so desired.

Note: Ackees are available at most Supermarket or Caribbean Supermarkets in the can

JAMAICA HOT & SPICY JERK PORK

5 lbs. -10 lbs. Lean Pork	5 ozs. Of Jerk Sauce	1 oz. Whole Spice grains/Pimento
5 Whole Garlic cloves	Fresh Scallions or leeks	1 Tablespoon Season Salt
1 Large Onion	Fresh Thyme	2 Large Onions
Lawry's Seasoned Salt	2 Tablespoon Whole Black Pepper (grind black pepper in a grinder)	
White Vinegar	2 Whole Jamaica Scotch Bonnet Pepper (cut into small pieces)	

Use Pork Shoulder or pork already sliced in thick 1-2 inch slices. Wash Pork in vinegar water, set aside.

Homemade Jerk Sauce:

1 Scotch Bonnet Pepper or Jalapenos; 2 Tsp. Salt

2 Tablespoon Black pepper; 2 Tb.spoon Ground Allspice

6 Sprigs of Fresh Thyme; 8 Cloves Garlic, finely chopped

2 Tsp. Sugar; Ground Nutmeg; Crushed Ginger

½ cup Olive Oil; 2 Cups Soy sauce; 1 lime, juiced

1 Cup orange juice; 1 Cup vinegar

Blend all ingredients together, use a blender. Be very careful. Wash hands thoroughly. Peppers can be very hot. Rub ingredients all over pork and set aside for at least 3 hours or leave in refrigerator overnight to marinate. Store the unused portion of the sauce in a Jar for use later.

Cooking: Light Charcoal Grill. Let the fire burn down until the flames subsides (You need the heat, not the flames). Add the pork directly on the grill and cover. Occasionally turn over and over to prevent burning. After the pork is thoroughly cooked. Sprinkle 1 cup of Jamaican Red Stripe Beer over pork and cover and let it simmer for another 5 minutes. Remove from grill and serve.

Note: The same process can be done by baking in the oven until thoroughly cooked. Or you can also use a Gas Grill.

JAMAICAN REGGAE STYLE JERK CHICKEN:

2 Whole chickens (3-4 lbs. each)

2 oz. Traditional Jerk Sauce

6 cloves whole garlic

4 Med. Onions

Salt to taste

2 tablespoon Black Pepper

1 Tablespoon Whole pimento grains

few springs of fresh thyme, few stalks scallion

PREPARATION:

Cut chicken in 2 halves, Wash chicken in vinegar and water, set aside. In bowl, dice onions in small pieces, crush scallion and cut in small pieces, about ½ inch. Crush pimento and add to mixture, peal garlic and crush with a rolling pin, add to mix, stir together.

Sprinkle chicken quarters with salt and black pepper, rub ½ of the Jerk Sauce over the Chicken, put in bowl with the ingredients. Rub ingredients all over the chicken. Cover tightly with plastic wrap and set aside for two hours. Note you could also marinate overnight before cooking. Cook on Barbeque Grill, Gas Grill, Charcoal Grill or in an Oven. Turn occasionally on each side until thoroughly cooked and brown in color.

Note: You can add Scotch Bonnet Pepper to your portion to suit your own taste if you like it hot. Use your discretion.

Serve with your favorite food: Festival, Rice, or Vegetables.

JAMAICAN PEPPER STEAK:

3 Lbs. Sirloin Steak (cut lengthwise ½" thick)

1 Tablespoon freshly g   1 tablespoon black ground black pepper 2/3 cups Red Wine

2 Tablespoon Beef   1 can consommé soup

Consommé soup1 The   1 Med. Onion 2 Tablespoon butter

¼ Cup Jamaican Rum

A few sprigs of Thyme and Scallion

PREPARATION:

Sprinkle ground black pepper on steak so that it is heavily coated. Let stand at room temperature for 30 minutes. Combine wine and consommé soup and set aside. Melt butter in a large skillet. When very hot cook steak over heat for 5 minutes, stirring constantly. Reduce heat and let steak cook until done, to your taste. Stir wine and consommé into skillet and remaining ingredients, including onions, thyme and scallion. Cover and cook for another 10 minutes. Serve hot.

JAMAICAN ROASTED AND STUFFED BREADFRUIT

Use one fit and breadfruit, not green, but yellow in color. With a sharp pointed knife, cut the stem out of the breadfruit. Use the knife to pierce the center of the breadfruit, enough to allow steam to escape while cooking. Make a slight cross cut in the bottom of the breadfruit; this will also release the steam.

Place the breadfruit on top of charcoal grill. Turn occasionally until thoroughly cooked. Remove from the heat and let cool. Scrape the black off the breadfruit then remove the skin. Cut the breadfruit in half, lengthwise, remove the heart from both sides. Slice lengthwise. Serve with meat or cooked fish.

CHICKEN PARMESAN:

4 Boneless/skinless Chicken Breast
halves, 1-1/2 Lbs.

2 Cups Tomato Pasta sauce

Salt & freshly ground pepper

¾ Cup Italian Style Bread Crumbs

¾ Cup Grated Parmesan Cheese

Enough Spaghetti for 4 servings

2-3 Tablespoon. Olive Oil

1/3 Cup All Purpose Flour

2 Eggs

1 Cup Shredded Mozzarella Cheese

In Bowl place ½ Teaspoon salt, ¼ Teaspoon Black Pepper and flour. Let it stand. In a separate bowl, beat the eggs until frothy. In a third bowl combine breadcrumbs & parmesan. Place chicken between two pieces of wax paper and pound with a mallet or rolling pin until flattened. Sprinkle both sides of the chicken breast with salt and black pepper, and then lightly dredge in seasoned flour. Shake off excess. Dip chicken in egg mixture, coat completely, and then dredge chicken in breadcrumbs mixture evenly on both sides. Heat oil over medium heat, place chicken in skillet and cook on both sides until golden brown (approx. 3 minutes per side) Put chicken breasts in baking tin and bake until cooked about 15 minutes. Spoon tomato sauce over chicken and sprinkle with Mozzarella Cheese. Return to oven until cheese is melted.

Serve with Spaghetti.

BARBECUE BEEF SPARE RIBS

2 Slabs Beef Spare Ribs	16 Oz's. Barbecue Sauce
4 Cloves Garlic (crushed)	Few Sprigs Fresh Thyme
1 Tablespoon Paprika	1 Teaspoon Garlic Powder
1 Cup Jamaican Rum	1 Lemon
1 Teaspoon Salt	1 Teaspoon Black Pepper
1 14 oz can Beef Broth	1 Medium Onion (cut small)

PREPARATIONS:

Wash Ribs and remove excess fat from the back of the ribs. In a separate container, add the Crushed Garlic Cloves, Paprika, Salt, Black Pepper, Thyme and Onion. Mix well together. Next lay the ribs flat on a cutting board and rub all the seasoning thoroughly over the ribs.

Heat the oven at 360 degrees. Line a large Baking Pan with aluminum foil. Lay the Ribs, bone side down. Open the can of Beef Broth and spread evenly over the ribs. Cover and bake for approximately 1 hour. Check occasionally and base if you have to. Cook until meat is tender. Remove from oven and extract or skim off excess fat. Put the barbecue sauce in a small container. Use a Food Brush or a spoon to spread the sauce evenly over the ribs. Return to the oven for another 10 minutes. Remove from oven and sprinkle the rum over the ribs; return to the oven for another 5 minutes. Remove from oven and serve.

OXTAIL STEW

2-1/2 – 3 Lbs. Jointed Oxtail (cut at the joint)

1/4 Tablespoon Seasoned Salt	1 Tablespoon Paprika
1 Tablespoon Soy Sauce	4 Cloves of Garlic
3 Sprigs of Thyme	Dash of Oregano
1 Tablespoon Browning	1 Medium Onion
8 Oz's. Butter Beans	

PREPARATION

Place Oxtail in a bowl. wash the meat and trim the fat. Peel Onions and cut up in thin ring slices. Crush the garlic cloves. Add all ingredients (except the butter beans to the meat and rub the Seasoning all over the Meat. Add the Food Browning and the Soy Sauce and let it sit at room temperature for at least 1 hour to marinate.

Heat 1 tablespoon of cooking oil in the pot and add the Oxtail. Let it simmer over medium heat for 10 minutes, then add enough water to cover the meat. Allow it to cook until meat is tender. Stir occasionally to prevent sticking and burning. In a separate pot boil the Butter Beans until cooked, then add to the oxtail and allow it to simmer for another 10 minutes. Add more water if necessary for gravy and the remaining seasoning and let it simmer. Remove from heat Serve with rice, vegetable and salad. (Pre-cooked Butter Beans is sold in most supermarkets.)

SWEET & SOUR SPARERIBS:

One 2-1/2 to 3-1/2 Lbs. Slab Pork Spare Ribs

½ Teaspoon Salt

½ Cup Cornstarch

Vegetable oil for deep frying

1 Clove Garlic, chopped

¾ Cup Sugar

½ Cup Vinegar

¼ Cup Molasses

½ Cup Soy Sauce

1 Cup Pineapple juice

2 Med. Onions, cut in med. Size pcs.

1 Can Pineapple Chunks, drained

PREPARATIONS:

Boil spareribs and drain. Add fresh water and bring to a boil. Add salt and cook until tender. Drain In paper bag, add corn starch and shake spare ribs until all pieces are covered. Fry in deep fryer, remove from oil. In separate saucepan, add all the other ingredients, simmer for two minutes. Add onions and pineapple chunks, cook for 5 to 10 more minutes and serve.

CHICKEN WITH BROCCOLI

4 Large Chicken Breasts

1 Small Onion, sliced

Fresh Broccoli

Fresh Thyme

3 Cubes Chicken Stock

2 Stalks Celery, diced

Black Pepper to taste

Assemble: Cut chicken into fairly large chunks (1-1/2 inch thick) Line casserole dish with chicken. Dot broccoli between chicken chunks. Season to taste. Pour sauce over chicken and broccoli.

To Make the Sauce, you will need the following:

1 Cup grated Cheddar Cheese; 2 Tablespoon Soy Sauce; 1 Can Cream of Chicken soup; 1/3rd Cup Evaporated Milk and ¾ Cup mayonnaise; 1 Teaspoon Lemon Juice.

After combining all of the ingredients, heat over low heat in a saucepan until it comes to a boil and thickens. Pour over chicken in casserole.

Topping: Combine 1 Cup of Bread Crumbs with 1 Tablespoon of Butter or Margarine. Spread topping over the mixture in the Casserole and bake at 350 degrees for approximately20-25 minutes.

FRICASSEED CHICKEN

1 Chicken (5 – 6 lbs.)

2 Large Onions (chopped)

3 Medium Beef Tomatoes

1 Clove Garlic, finely chopped

1 Unbroken Scotch Bonnet Pepper

1 Teaspoon Black Pepper

1 Tablespoon Season Salt

1 Tablespoon of powdered Ginger

½ Teaspoon Paprika

Couple pieces of Fresh Thyme

DIRECTIONS:

Cut up the Chicken in fairly large pieces. Wash the chicken in vinegar water. Drain off all the water. Next, Season the Chicken with the Onion, Thyme, Pepper, Salt and powdered ginger. Cover and set in refrigerator overnight. Next day, remove all seasoning. Heat enough oil in a skillet to brown chicken on both sides. Lower the heat. Remove some of the oil and add chopped onions, tomatoes, garlic salt and unbroken pepper, paprika and ¼ Cup of water. Cover and let it simmer until cooked. adding very small amount of water until chicken is cooked.

CHICKEN & RICE:

1 Chicken 3-4 Lbs.

½ Cup Water

1 Bottle Jamaican Red Stripe Beer

12 small Plum tomatoes

Oil for frying

2 Cloves Garlic

1 Tablespoon Salt or Season Salt

1 Can Red Pimentos

2 Cups of Rice

1 14 Oz. Can Red Pimentos

2 Cups Par Boiled Rice

1 Medium Onion

1 Medium Bell Green Pepper

Black Pepper

Yellow Food Coloring

PREPARATION:

Cut chicken in quarters, chop Onions, Crush the Garlic, and season the chicken, add the black pepper and salt or Season Salt. Cover and let it stand for at least one hour to allow the season to soak in. Fry the chicken until it has a brown color, turning constantly to prevent burning. Next add the water; the beer, tomatoes and green pepper. Cook over low heat until chicken is almost cooked. Wash the rice and add the food coloring,   then combine it with the chicken and cook until rice and chicken are tender. Pour in serving dish and decorate with red pimentos.

CHICKEN IN RED WINE SAUCE

One Chicken, 4-5 lbs.

(Quartered)

½ Pint Red Wine, or sweet sherry

4 Cloves of Garlic

4 Oz. Tomato Paste

1 Med. Green Bell Pepper

¼ cup stuffed olives

6 Med. Size Onions

2 Medium Tomatoes (plum)

1 Can Chicken Gravy (8 ozs.)

4 Oz. Margarine

Bay Leaf or Oregano

2Tablespoons Flour

8 oz. can mushroom

Salt and Black Pepper to taste

few Pimentos grains

Hard boiled eggs

Note: You can make the chicken gravy by boiling the backs and necks of the chicken. Strained and set aside.

Wash chicken thoroughly with lime or vinegar. Crush the garlic, cut up the Onions, small, and add the salt and black pepper. Season chicken and set aside for about two hours or overnight. If left overnight, cover and place it in the refrigerator.

Fry chicken to a light brown color, turning on both sides., Place some of the onions in saucepan with 1 bay leaf or oregano, 2 cloves of garlic, 4 oz. butter and 1/2 tomato paste. Add two tablespoon of flour, 6 ozs. Red wine or sherry and four ozs. liquid from can of mushrooms. Add 4 ozs. of chicken gravy and 4 ozs. boiling water, then the chicken. Cover and cook over medium heat for 30 minutes. Add the rest of the chicken gravy to the sauce; add chopped green bell pepper and two medium tomatoes, skinned and chop the tomatoes; then add a small amount of season salt. Add very thinly sliced mushrooms and olives on top. Return to heat for 15 minutes. Serve warm.

STRING BEAN CASSEROLE:

¼ Cup Mushrooms	1 Med. Onion
(Sauté in ¼ cup butter)	Add two cans cream of mushroom soup
¾ Cup Grated sharp cheddar Cheese	1 Tablespoon Soy Sauce
1/8 Teaspoon Tabasco Sauce	½ Teaspoon Black Pepper
1 Teaspoon Salt	2 packs French- style frozen string beans

Cook beans until tender, and crunchy. In separate casserole cook all ingredients until it thickens. Add string beans. Add 5 oz. thinly sliced water chestnuts. Cover with sauce. Sprinkle ½ cup blanched slivered almonds on top. Bake at 375º for 20 minutes.

POTATO & ONION CASSEROLE

4 Large potatoes, peeled
sliced very thin

½ Teaspoon freshly ground black
Pepper

½ Cup Heavy Cream

2 Tablespoons grated Parmesan Cheese

1-1/2 Cup thinly sliced onions

2 Teaspoon salt

5 Tablespoons Butter or Margarine

½ Cup dry white wine

2 Tablespoons dry bread crumbs

PREPARATION:

In a buttered 9 inch Pyrex dish, arrange layers of sliced potatoes and onions and sprinkle each layer with salt and pepper, dot with half the butter/margarine. In separate container, mix together wine and cream and pour over top, then sprinkle with bread crumbs and cheese and dot with remaining butter. Bake at 375º F for 45 minutes or until potatoes are cooked. Serve: cut in pie shape wedges.

JAMAICA
FRUIT PUNCHES

FRUIT COCKTAIL/FRUIT SALAD

2 Lg. Sweet Oranges

2 cups Fresh Ripe Papaya (diced)

2 Large Tangerines

1 Can Sweetened Condensed Milk

1 Cup Pink Marshmallows

½ Cup Grapefruit juice

1 Lg. Grapefruit

2 Ripe Mangos

1 Ripe Banana

½ Cup Pineapple Chunks

1 Cup Orange Juice

DIRECTIONS:

Cut oranges in four quarters and remove the pulp. Peel the Tangerines and separate the pegs or pulp; Peel the grapefruit and remove the pulp. Peel the Banana and cut in ¼ inch thickness. Peel the Pineapple and cut in ¼ inch thickness. In a large bowl, combine all the fruits. Add the orange juice, grapefruit juice; marshmallows. Add sweetened Condensed Milk to taste. Refrigerate before serving.

FRUIT PLATTER MEDLEY

2 Cups Green Seedless Grapes

1 Medium Cantaloupe

1 Green Apple

1 Medium Honeydew

1 Lemon

2 Cups Red Seedless Grapes

1 Medium Ripe Papaya

1 Red Apple

½ of 1 Ripe Pineapple

1 Cup Blueberries

DIRECTIONS:

Wash all fruits thoroughly. Then remove the skin from the Papaya, Cantalope, Pineapple and Honeydew. Remove the stem from the Pineapple and set aside.

In a large Platter, set the Pineapple stem in the center. Slice all of the fruits into very thin slices. Do not remove the skin from the apples. Cut the apples lengthwise and remove the seeds. Arrange all the sliced fruits around the Pineapple stem. Sprinkle the juice of the Lemon evenly over the fruits. Refrigerate before serving.

JAMAICAN STYLE EGG NOG

12 Eggs (separated)   3 Cups Milk

½ cup granulated sugar   1 Cup Light whipped cream

4 ozs (1 Cup Jamaican Over-proof White Rum Cup Brandy or 1 Cup Scotch whisky

PREPARATION:

Beat egg yolks with a hand whisk or electric blender until thick and creamy.

Gradually beat in sugar. Next gradually stir in combined liquor.

Cover and chill. Before serving, gently stir in the milk and fold in the beaten egg

Whites, which is beaten to a smooth paste, and the whipped cream.

Serve over crushed ice.

JAMAICA BLUE MOUNTAIN COFFEE FLAVORED DRINK

¾ Pint strong Instant Blue Mountain coffee, brewed and cooled

2 Tablespoon granulated. Sugar   2 Egg Yolks

1 Pint Cold Milk   2 Egg white

Crushed Ice

PREPARATION: BEAT EGG YOLKS UNTIL FLUFFY.

Beat the egg yolks in a blender until fluffy. Place the coffee, milk, sugar and the beaten

Egg yolks into cocktail shaker and shake vigorously until mixture becomes frothy.

In separate Blender, beat the egg white at medium speed, vigorously into stiff peaks.

Put crushed ice in glasses and pour coffee mixture and half of the beaten egg whites

Over the ice. Lastly. Float the remaining egg white on top.

Note: Jamaica Blue Mountain Coffee can be obtained from most supermarkets or Caribbean food stores

ICED TEA - FRUIT PUNCH MEDLEY

6 Pints of boiling water

5 Teaspoon Lipton Tea mix

5 Teaspoon chopped fresh mint leaves

5 Med. Ripe Oranges

1-1/4 Cups light or dark Sugar

4 Medium Ripe Lemons

thinly cut Lemon slices

Picher of Cracked Ice

Pour boiling water on the tea and mint. Cover and let stand for ½ hour, then strain into a bowl. Stir in the sugar until dissolved. Juice the oranges and remove the seeds. Stir in the strained orange juice and the lemon juice and add some thinly peeled lemon rind. Add the sugar and stir vigorously. Let stand for 2 to 3 hours and then strain into punch bowl with some crushed ice. Garnish with thin slices of oranges and lemon.

JAMAICAN STYLE FRUIT PUNCH

INGREDIENTS:

2-1/2 Cups Orange Juice

1 Cup canned Jamaica Pineapple Juice

¼ Cup Lemon Juice

2 Cups Cold Water

½ Teaspoon Nutmeg

¼ Teaspoon Jamaica Allspice

1 Can of Fruit Cocktail in light syrup

5-6 whole cloves –to add a little spicy taste

4 Tablespoon Jamaican Honey

6 Whole Cloves

Picher with Crushed Ice

8 Ozs. Of Ginger Ale

3 Tablespoon grated ripe lemon rind

DIRECTIONS:

Combine all ingredients except ginger ale and ice. Let chill for at least 3 hours in the Refrigerator. Strain, and then add ginger ale, fruit cocktail and ice. Pour into punch bowl and garnish with thin slices of lemon and oranges.

Pour over ice in punch bowl glasses.

JAMAICAN CHRISTMAS SORREL DRINK

2 to 3 bunches of sorrel or 1 lb. fresh sorrel

1 Gal. of Boiling Water

Crushed Ginger

2 Cups of Jamaican White Rum

PREPARATION:

Strip the red blossoms from the stems, or buy the sorrel already stripped.

Place Sorrel in a large pot, add crushed ginger. Pour boiling water over sorrel and ginger, cover tightly and let it stand overnight. The liquid should be purple in color and a bit tangy. Add the rum and sweeten to taste.

JAMAICAN STYLE GINGER BEER

5 Oz. Fresh Jamaican Ginger

1 Cake Yeast

2-1/2 Cups granulated Sugar

¼ Cup Jamaican Honey

1 Egg White

2 Qtr. Water

¼ Cup Lime Syrup

Angostura Bitters

DIRECTIONS:

Peel and grate ginger; add water, sugar, honey and lime syrup and pour into a glass bowl.

Add yeast and egg white beat slightly. Let it stand in a cool place for 3 days. Pour off water without stirring and strain through a sieve. *Add more sugar to taste and a few drops* of Angostura Bitters. Bottle and refrigerate.

JAMAICAN STYLE RUM PUNCH

1 Cups Lime Juice (extract enough juice from fresh limes to make 1 cup

2 Cups Strawberry Syrup

3 Cups Jamaican White Over-proof Rum

4 Cups of Water

1 Teaspoon dried Pimento Grains

In a Large container, pour the Lime juice; Syrup; Rum; and Water. Stir/mix well together. Pour in Quart bottles and add a few pimento grains on top. Let it stand in a cool place for overnight before serving. Pour over ice in rum glasses.

Garnish glass with a slice of lemon

Note: This drink is for Adults. Drink responsibly -18 years or older.

SOUPS

PUMPKIN SOUP

2 Lbs. Pumpkin

(Rich yellow color, diced)

2 Lg. Stalks Scallion

1 Clove Garlic (crushed)

1 whole Scotch Bonnet Pepper

2 springs of fresh thyme

1/2 Lb. Lean Salted Beef

1-1/2 Lb. Beef Soup Meat

In Large pot, place salted beef in 2 quarts of water and boil until meat is almost cooked. Remove from heat and through off the salted water. Add 2 quarts of water then add the Soup beef meat and cook on medium heat until meat is tender. Add diced pumpkin, green pepper and boil until pumpkin is completely dissolved. Add the rest of the seasoning to taste. For a richer and thicker soup, add a coyote, 1 carrot, cut up, and a potato. .

BEEF SOUP WITH FRESH VEGETABLES:

1 Lb. Soup Meat (bone in center)

2 Stalks Fresh Scallions

1 Green Scotch Bonnet Pepper

2 Med. Size Potato

1 Chocho

2 Cups of Flour, 2 Tablespoon Cornmeal

1 Packet Grace Flavored Soup Mix (contains noodles 1.7 ozs.)

1 Med. Turnip

3 Cloves Garlic

1 Small Onion

1 Teaspoon Salt

1 Cocoa (Malagna)

1 lb. Pumpkin yellow in color

1 lb. Jamaican Yellow Yam

2 Med. Carrots

DIRECTIONS:

Wash Soup Meat and place it in 2 quarts of water, add garlic and salt Let boil on Med. Heat for at least 30 minutes.

Next: Dice the Pumpkin, Chocho, Turnip and Carrots into 1/2" thick pieces and add to meat. Let it boil until meat and vegetables are tender. In separate sauce pan pour in flour and cornmeal and a dash of salt to taste, mix well, then *add* ½ cup of water gradually into a pastry and mix the dough into a ball, set aside. Peal Yellow Yam, Potato, Malagna (Jamaica Cocoa) Cut in 4 pieces and add to the pot. Next, make the dumplings from the pastry flour and add to soup. Lastly add the Scallions, Chopped Onions and Soup Flavored Mix and the whole Scotch Bonnet Pepper and let it cook for another 30 minutes or to taste. (Do not break the Pepper in the soup. Remove the Pepper before serving.

OXTAIL SOUP:

2-1/2 Lb. Oxtail, jointed

¼ pint dried broad beans,

or canned butter beans

6 pimento grains

2 springs fresh thyme

¼ tsp. salt

2 Med. Carrots

2 Tablespoon dry sherry

3 stalks scallion

1 whole scotch bonnet pepper

1 small onion, finely chopped

1 clove garlic

In large saucepan place Oxtail, carrots and beans with sufficient water to cover well. Boil until meat is tender. Add garlic and continue boiling for about 20 minutes. Skim off fat from the top. Add more water to make sufficient amount of soup. Add all seasoning to the soup and continue to cook. Lower heat and let it simmer. Add Sherry. Serve hot.

JAMAICA PEPPERPOT SOUP

2-1/2 Lbs. Spinach, chopped small

1 Doz. Okras, cut in small rings

1 lb. kale, chopped

1 whole green cayenne pepper

1 medium onion cut up small

2 cloves garlic, crushed

½ cup coconut milk

1 small garden eggplant, chopped

½ lb. coco (malagna)

1-1/2 lb. Soup Meat

½ lb. salted pigs tail

3 stalks scallion

2 springs of thyme

DIRECTIONS:

Precook salted Pigs Tail; remove from the heat and through off the water.

In large pot, add 4 quarts of water add the soup meat and crushed garlic. Boil until meat is tender. Add coco. Add all vegetables; Pigs Tail and all seasoning. Cook until all the vegetables are soft and tender. Simmer until soup begins to thickened, then add Coconut Milk and cook for an additional 10 to 15 minutes. Serve hot.

JAMAICA RED PEAS SOUP

INGREDIENTS

1 Pint Red Peas

4 Quarts Water

1-1/2 Lb. Soup Meat (Beef)

2 Small White Potaoes

½ Lb. All Purpose Flour

½ Lb. Cocoa (Veg)

3 Stalks Escallion (Green)

1 Sprig Thyme

1 Whole Unbroken Green Hot

 Pepper

PREPARATION:

Wash Meat, remove fat. In separate container, wash the peas thoroughly. Place in pot with 4 quarts of water. Cook over medium heat for 25 minutes or until peas is soft. Add meat and allow it to boil until the peas and the meat are both tender. Add of the all vegetables. (Cut the potatoes in halves).

Cut the cocoa in quarters. Cut the vegetables in small pieces and add to the soup.

In a separate bowl, mix the flour with a pinch of salt. Add water in small amounts and mix the dough. Knead the dough until it looks like Pizza dough. Pinch off small amounts and roll in the palms of your hands into dumplings. Add to the pot and let it simmer for 45 minutes. Add the remaining Seasoning; Scallion, Thyme; the whole green Scotch Bonnet pepper. (Do not break the pepper).

Cook on low heat. Stir occasionally. Remove from heat when cooked serve in a soup bowl.

DESERTS:
CAKES PUDDING

RIPE BANANA BREAD

2 CUPS FLOUR

1 CUP LIGHT BROWN SUGAR

½ CUP RAISINS

1 TEASPOON NUTMEG

3 LARGE VERY RIPE BANANAS,

1 TEASPOON CINNAMON

¼ TEASPOON SALT

¼ LB. BUTTER

½ CUP MILK

1 EGG BEATEN

1 TEASPOON BAKING POWDER

1 TEASPOON BAKING SODA

2 TEASPOON VANILLA

¼ TEASPOON ALLSPICE

PREPARATION:

Cream butter and sugar together. Beat egg separately until fluffy and add to butter and sugar mixture. Crush the bananas with a spoon or spatula and add it to the mixture. Next sieve flour and baking powder, cinnamon, nutmeg, salt and allspice into mixture. Gradually add milk and vanilla while constantly stirring. Lastly, add the raisins and stir. Spread mixture evenly in greased shallow baking tin and bake at 350 degrees for 20 minutes.

JAMAICA EASTER BUN

2 YEAST CAKE

1 WHOLE NUTMEG (Grated)

1 EGG

¼ LB. RAISINS (CHOPPED)

1 CUP BROWN SUGAR

4 CUPS FLOUR

1 CUP WATER

1 TEASPOON SALT

¼ LB. CRYSTALIZED CHERRIES (chopped)

1-1/2 PT. MILK (BOILED)

½ LB. BUTTER

¼ LB. CITRON (CHOPPED)

1 TEASPOON CINNAMON

PINCH ¼ TEASPOON ALLSPICE

DIRECTIONS:

Dissolve yeast cake in small amount of water. Warm milk until it boils, and then adds a Cup of water. Then place butter, sugar, salt and spice in a bowl and pour milk and water over the mixture. Beat the egg with a whisk or fork and add it to the mixture. Sieve half of the flour into the mixture and stir well. Next stir in the yeast and the Remaining flour to make stiff dough. Cover with cheese cloth or similar, a linen napkin Would work just as well. Let rise at room temperature until the dough is double in size. Grease and flour loaf baking pan put dough into baking pan and bake at 350 degrees until bun leave the side of the pan or appears cooked.

COCONUT BUNS

1 CUP GRATED COCONUT   ½ LB. FLOUR

½ LB. SUGAR   ¼ LB. BUTTER MARGARINE

1 EGG   1 TEASPOON BAKING POWDER

1 CUP MILK

PREPARATION:

Grease baking pan and four lightly, dust off excess flour. In a separate bowl, sieve the flour and baking powder together. Cream the butter and sugar separately until fluffy. Beat the egg and add a little milk. Add liquid and flour, by degrees, making a stiff dough. Mix in the coconut. Place dough in small heaps on greased and floured baking sheet. Bake in oven for 20 minutes at around 375 degrees.

JAMAICA BULLA CAKE

3 CUPS FLOUR

1 TEASPOON BAKING POWDER

¼ TEASPOON SALT

SUGAR INTO THICK SYRUP

¼ TEASPOON NUTMEG

½ TEASPOON GRATED GINGER

½ TEASPOON ALLSPICE

10 OZS. DARK BROWN SUGAR

SUFFICIENT WATER TO BLEND

2 TABLESPOON MELTED BUTTER

1 TEASPOON CINNAMON

PREPARATION:

Sieve all dry ingredients together. Pour the thick sugar syrup into the center then add the melted butter and blend together.

Place on well-floured cutting board. Pat with your hands to a thickness of ¼ inch. Use a regular size drinking glass to cut dough around the mouth of the glass in circles. Or use a large cookie cutter. Remove from the cutting board with a spatula and place on greased floured baking tin. Bake for 20 minutes in 375 degrees oven. Remove from heat and let it cool.

JAMAICA CHRISTMAS RUM CAKE:

INGREDIENTS:

1 LB. All-Purpose Flour	1 Doz. Eggs (LG)
½ LB. Butter	½ LB. Margarine
1 LB. Sugar (Light Brown)	1 Teaspoon Allspice
3 Teaspoon Baking Powder	¼ Teaspoon Salt
1 Teaspoon grated Nutmeg	2 Teaspoon Ground Cinnamon
Grated Rind of 1 Lime	2 Teaspoon Vanilla
Burnt Sugar for coloring	

DIRECTIONS FOR PREPARATION OF FRUITS

2 lbs. Raisins	¼ lb. Pecan Nuts
½ lb. Currants	¼ lb. Mixed peel
1 lb. Seedless Prunes	½ lb. Cherries
1 Bottle Rich Port Wine (750 ML)	1/4 lb. Dates
2 teaspoon Vanilla	1 Pint Rum (White)
1 Cup Sherry Wine	

In a Blender, chop raisins, prunes, cherries into small pieces, pour into a large jar, add currants, pour half of the rum and half of the port wine and sherry over the fruits, cover tightly and steep for at least one month prior to baking.

Baking: Assemble all your ingredients grease and flour lightly (2) 9x10 baking pans. (Line the bottom of the baking pans with wax paper).

Use a mixer. Cream Butter, Margarine and sugar at slow/medium speed until fluffy. Gradually add two eggs at a time to the mixture, (break the eggs in a separate small container to be sure the eggs are good), pour into mixture. Add 2 eggs at a time, sieve two tablespoon of flour on top of the eggs, then fold in with wooden spoon, in a moon over motion. Note; Mix the same way until all the eggs are used. Follow this procedure through the entire mixing process. Add fruits in small amounts with a spoon of flour and fold into the mixture to desired thickness. Next, add chopped nuts, cinnamon, allspice, baking powder salt. Be sure mixture is thick; gradually add burnt sugar by degrees, turning over to fold it in to desired color. (Not too dark).

Last, Pour gently into baking pans. Bake in preheated oven at 325 degrees for ½ hour; reduce heat to 300 degrees for the remainder. Baked when the cake leaves the side of the baking pans. (Do not open oven before the cake is baked to avoid the cake collapsing).

When the cake is baked, remove from oven and add some of the remaining wine or rum. Let cool before serving.

JAMAICA SWEET POTATO PUDDING

2 Lbs. Sweet Potatoes (uncooked)

½ Lb. Brown Sugar

1 Teaspoon Cinnamon

1 Tablespoon Butter

1 Quart Hot Water

3-1/2 Cups Coconut Milk

2 Teaspoon Vanilla

¼ Teaspoon grated Nutmeg

1 Coconut (grated fine)

1 Tablespoon Currants

1 Teaspoon Powdered

1 Teaspoon Ginger

PREPARATION:

Grease a 10" baking pan and slightly dust flour in the pan, shake off excess flour.

Grate Sweet Potatoes (do not use shredder side of grater use the smaller size shredder)

Combine grated potatoes, Coconut Milk, Sugar, Spices, Raisins, and Currants, add vanilla and 1 tablespoon butter. Pour into greased baking pan, baked in moderate oven until the pudding is cooked (approx. 1 hour)

Note: Coconut milk can be obtained by grating the meat of the Coconut add water and extract the juice. Run it through a strainer to remove of the pulp. You can also substitute with coconut milk sold in your neighborhood Super markets that carry Jamaican Products).

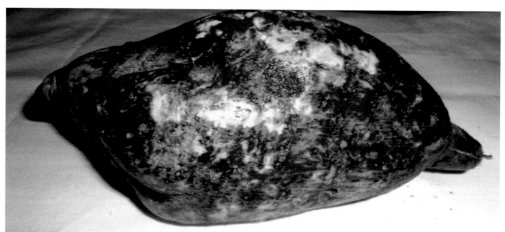

CORNMEAL & SWEET POTATO PUDDING

2 Cups Cornmeal	2 Teaspoons Vanilla
2 Cups Sweet Potato (raw, grated)	¼ Teaspoon Nutmeg
1 Cup Brown Sugar	1 Teaspoon Cinnamon
1 Med. Size Coconut (grated)	1 Tablespoon Butter
Expressed 3 cups coconut milk from 1 Coconut)	
½ Teaspoon Salt	½ Cup raisins
2 Tablespoons All Purpose Flour	

PREPARATION:

Add Sugar to Milk and mix until sugar is almost dissolved.

Add cornmeal and gradually mixed well, then grated potato and flour, Mix thoroughly. Add the spices, such as the vanilla, cinnamon and nutmeg, raisins and salt. Mix thoroughly. Pour mixture into greased/floured baking pan.

Dot top of the mixture with butter and bake at 375 degrees F for roughly 1-1/2 hours or until cooked

JAMAICA YELLOW YAM PUDDING

INGREDIENTS:

1 Cup Yellow Yam (grated raw)	½ Cup Butter	1-1/2 Cups Breadcrumbs
1 Cup Sugar	½ Cup Flour (all purpose)	2 Teaspoon Baking Powder
1/3 Cup of burnt Sugar	Grated rind of 1 green lime	¼ Teaspoon Nutmeg

1 Cup fruits- Use the fruits already soaked in rum and a little wine; Add Raisins,

currants, mixed peel and a few nuts.

PREPARATION:

Use a fork, beat yam slightly after it is gratered, and then mix all

The other ingredients together. Pour in a baking ten and steam in a Pudding Steamer for about 2 hours, or place in oven at 250ºF. Coverer and bake for at least 3 hours. Serve cool.

JAMAICA CARROT PUDDING

½ Cup Butter

1 Cup shifted All Purpose Flour

½ Teaspoon Baking Soda

¼ Teaspoon Baking Powder

1 Tablespoon Water

1 Cup grated raw carrots

1 Tablespoon Lemon rind

½ Cup Brown Sugar

1 Egg

1 Cup Seedless Raisins (chopped)

¼ Teaspoon Cinnamon

½ Teaspoon Salt

½ Teaspoon Grated Nutmeg

¼ Teaspoon Chopped Nuts

PREPARATION:

Cream butter and sugar; combine slightly beaten egg and water then stir in butter and sugar ingredients. Next, Stir in the carrots, lemon rind and raisins. Shift together dry ingredients and add to mixture; add nuts. Pour mixture into greased and floured baking tin, cover with foil tightly, place in oven on the second shelf. In a separate baking tin at least 14" wide, pour enough water to cover the bottom about half of the tin. Place pan with the water on the bottom shelf of the oven directly under the pudding and let it steam-cook for 1 hour or until thoroughly cooked.

Note: steam cooking keeps the moisture in.

JAMAICA CUSTARD PIE

INGREDIENTS:

½ Cup Milk   3 Egg Yolks, beaten

½ Cup Sugar   6 Egg Whites, beaten stiff

6 Tablespoon Flour   4 Tablespoon Jamaica White Rum

1 Tablespoon butter

PREPARATION:

Dissolve sugar, milk, stirring constantly, add flour and stir until smooth and thick. Remove from heat, add butter and egg yolks. Blend in thoroughly, then fold in egg whites and the rum. Pour into a baking dish and bake for 20 minutes in 350ºF oven. Then turn heat up for another 10 minutes. Serve at once. Serve 6 people.

ORANGE RING CAKE

INGREDIENTS:

¼ Lb. Butter

1-1/2 Cup All Purpose Flour

1 Cup Sour Cream

2 Teaspoons Cinnamon

1 Teaspoon Vanilla

Pinch of Salt

1 Cup Brown Sugar

1 Egg

Juice one medium size orange remove the seeds

1 Teaspoon grated Orange Rind

1 Cup Raisins

1 Teaspoon Baking Soda

DIRECTIONS:

Cream butter and sugar. Add 1 Egg, unbeaten and then add the Sour Cream. Nest, add raisins and dried ingredients to the mixture. Pour into a greased ring mound baking pan. Bake in moderate oven at about 360ºF. Remove from oven when cooked and sprinkle with orange juice and top off with brown sugar.

PINEAPPLE UPSIDE DOWN CAKE

INGREDIENTS:

4 Eggs (separate the white from the Yolk) (let eggs stand at room temperature)

1-1/2 Cup Sifted cake flour	10 Crystalized Cherries
½ Cup Butter	1 Teaspoon Baking Powder
1 Cup Light Brown Sugar	¼ teaspoon salt
1 Cup Granulated Sugar	1 Tablespoon Butter (melted)
1 Teaspoon Almond extract	1 Cup Heavy Cream (whipped)
½ Cup chopped pecans	1 Can Jamaica Pineapple slices (drained) 20 ozs.

Grease and flour a 10 inch baking tin. Preheat oven to 325ºF.

PREPARATION:

Melt half cup of butter over low heat; remove from heat. Sprinkle brown sugar over butter. Arrange pineapple slices to cover bottom of skillet. Distribute pecans and cherries around pineapple and set aside.

Sift flour with baking powder and salt together. At high speed, beat egg whites until soft peaks are formed. Gradually add the granulated sugar; Mix well after each addition. Beat until a stiff peaks is formed.

In small bowl, use an electric mixer set at high speed to beat egg yolks until very thick and yellow. Using an under and over motion, gently fold egg yolks and flour mixture into beaten egg whites until mixture is combined. Fold in 1 tablespoon butter and the almond extract. Spread evenly over pineapple in skillet. Bake for 30-45 minutes or until done.

COCONUT CREAM PIE

1 Cup Granulated Sugar

½ Cup Cornstarch

¼ Teaspoon Salt

3 Cups Hot Milk

3 Egg Yolks (beaten)

1 Teaspoon Vanilla

½ Teaspoon Almond Extract

2 Cups grated fresh Coconut

1- 9" Baked Pie Shell

1 Cup Heavy Cream

DIRECTIONS:

Combine sugar, cornstarch and salt, gradually add to milk in medium saucepan, stirring until smooth. Bring to boil over medium heat for two minutes. Remove from heat. Stir some of the hot mixture into egg yolks, then combine the rest in saucepan, cook over low heat, stirring until it boils and the mixture thickens (about 5 minutes). Pour into bowl, stir in extract and half of coconut. Cover with wax paper and place in refrigerator for 1 hour. Pour into pie shell and refrigerate for 3 hours.

Spread whip cream over filling and top with remaining coconut. (Note: you may substitute fresh coconut with 2; 7 oz. cans packaged flaked coconut.

TRIFFLE

Essentials: Select a Pyrex Dish about 9" x 2" deep.

Ingredients needed

1 Sponge Cake (9"x5-1/2" by1-1/2" thick, Cut ½ inch thick

9 Lg. Egg Yolks (lightly beaten)	1 Tablespoon Custard Powder
1 Pint Heavy Cream, whipped	(1) 15 oz. Can of Fruit Cocktail (drained)
2 Slices of canned pineapple	1 Tablespoon slivered toasted almonds
2 Teaspoon Vanilla	½ Cup Condensed Milk
1 Cup Evaporated Milk	1 Teaspoon of rind from a green lime
1 Cup Milk; ½ Cup Sherry Wine;	2 Tablespoon Jamaican Rum

1Tablespoon Red & Green Candied Cherries

DIRECTIONS:

Place cubed sponge cake into a bowl and sprinkle with cherries. Set aside for the cake to absorb the Liquor thoroughly. Do not crumple cake. Whip cream and set aside in refrigerator. Slightly beaten egg yolks. Combine all three milks, Evaporated Milk, Condensed Milk, and Regular Milk, then add a sliver of lime rind and bring to a boil over medium heat. Remove from heat and add the slightly beaten egg yolks. Place on very low heat, stirring constantly with a wooden spoon for roughly 10 minutes. Remove from the heat and add creamed custard powder while continually stirring until custard becomes stiff. Cool then add vanilla and 2 tablespoon Jamaican Rum.

Pour sufficient custard mix into Pyrex dish enough to cover the bottom. Add soaked sponge cake evenly on bottom. Next Spread fruit cocktail and pineapple bits over cake. Sprinkle with toasted almonds. Then pour on the rest of the custard and place in refrigerator until Custard sets well. Topped with whipped cream and decorate with candied cherries

Keep refrigerated until serving time.

Printed in the United States
by Baker & Taylor Publisher Services